CW00421718

LACQUER MINIATURES

·

FEDOSKINO

MASTERPIECES OF RUSSIAN FOLK ART

N. KRESTOVSKAYA

LACQUER
MINIATURES

·

FEDOSKINO

INTER
BOOK

INTERBOOK. MOSCOW. 1995

Editorial Board of collection *Masterpieces of Russian Folk Art*:

Irina Boguslavskaya, Doctor of Sciences (Art), Head, Folk Art Department, the State Russian Museum

Irina Ukhanova, Doctor of Sciences (History) Sector Head, Department of History of Russian Culture, the State Hermitage

Nadezhda Krestovskaya, Senior Researcher, the State Russian Museim

Gennady Popov, Director, "Interbook-Business" Publishing House

Text by:
Nadezhda Krestovskaya

Illustrations compiled by:
Nadezhda Krestovskaya, State Russian Museum
Marie Sarkisova, State History Museum
Liudmila Pirogova, All-Russia Museum of Decorative, Applied and Folk Art

Photography by:
Vladimir Dorokhov and Evgeni Gavrilov

Layout and book design by:
Juri Leonov

Translated by:
Liudmila Lezhneva

ISBN 5-7664-1048-4   © Interbook. 1995

"Lying on a sofa in a grey house suit, nestled in German pillows.... he used to fiddle with some small object, his old black snuffbox, its lacquer gone tarnished...." That was how *Russkie Vedomosti* (The Russian Gazette) described Russian writer Ivan Turgenev in 1884. History has, surprisingly, preserved for us Turgenev's favorite plaything. When leaving, for the last time, Russia for Paris, where he was not allowed to smoke or snuff tobacco, Turgenev left his snuffbox as a souvenier with his friend, writer Yakov Polonsky. The Polonsky family carefully stored that relic, which was then transferred to the Pushkin House, that is, the Museum of the Russian Literature Institute. Turgenev's snuffbox is still on display at that museum. It is a small oblong black lacquer box, the size of two matchboxes. Its lid is decorated with a picture of a sledge driven by three horses, flying along the snow-laden field. Smartly dressed rosy-cheeked young ladies are riding in the sledge, with a spirited coachman whipping the heated horses. Inside the purple-lacquer coated lid bears a semi-obliterated picture of a gold double-headed eagle with the letters "F. A. L." (Alexander Lukutin's factory trademark) underneath.

The village of Fedoskino, situated 40km north of Moscow on the picturesque banks of the Ucha River, is Russia's oldest centre of lacquer miniature painting. At least half of the inhabitants of this village and the neighbouring ones are in one way or another connected with the traditional craft. The secrets of making and painting papier-mache lacquers have for 200 years now been passed from one generation to another.

The French word "papier-mache" (literally "chewed paper") is well-rooted in the Russian language. Several layers of pasted cardboard, boiled in linseed oil and then repeatedly dried in a hot oven, form an original material — hard as wood, light and waterproof — that can be sawed, polished, primed and lacquered. In the 18th through the 19th century papier-mache was widely used to make sundry items from peaks for the Russian army headdress to trays, tables and even chandeliers. Needless to say, all sorts of papier-mache caskets and boxes used to store matches, stamps, cards, glasses and above all snuff were immensely popular.

The fashion for snuffing had come from the West and was, naturally, at first confined to high society. Tobacco was brought from afar and was very expensive, and for that reason snuffboxes, too, were made of costly materials, such as ivory, tortoiseshell, porcelain, precious metals and gems. The best jewellers were commissioned to make snuffboxes, which at times cost a fortune. By the end of the 18th century snuffing had become widespread — every shop-assistant thought it a matter of self-esteem to have a snuffbox near at hand. Demand for inexpensive mass-produced snuffboxes was on the rise, and papier-mache proved a suitable material. A host of small factories engaged in making snuffboxes in Russia at that time. Among others, Moscow merchant Petr Korobov also founded one such factory.

Certain papers of the Korobov factory proprietors, which have survived among 19th century Finance Ministry documents, shed light on the date of the foundation of the factory. Korobov's daughter wrote in the 1820 factory performance record that her father had purchased land for the factory in the village of Danilkovo on the Ucha bank opposite Fedoskino in 1796. The same papers give information about the factory's output, stating that in 1811 it produced 560 dozen snuffboxes "with kunststuck" (ornaments) and 145 dozen plain snuffboxes. The factory had a personnel of 30 local hired peasants.

Petr Korobov's factory was the first in the Moscow region. The neighbouring Marfino and Troitsk volosts (now the Mytishchi district) followed suit by launching similar productions. Seven kilometres away from Fedoskino, on the other bank of the Klyazma River is the village of Zhostovo and within another kilometre, the village of Ostashkovo. F. F. Gusarov, M. G. Kozlov and the Vishnyakov Brothers opened their workshops there after 1810. Kiril Pansky of the petty bourgeoisie opened a snuff-box-making factory in the village of Starogorie. A large lacquer centre thus formed around Fedoskino and Zhostovo. As a rule, a lacquer workshop employed ten to twelve craftsmen, including several turners who worked the blanks for snuffboxes, primers, lacquerers, three to five painters and a couple of apprentices. Such a workshop annually produced up to 1,000 dozen snuffboxes.

However, let us return to Petr Korobov's factory. No exact figures on its earliest products have survived. According to legend, Korobov went to Germany to visit Johann Stobwasser's factory in Braunschweig and brought back round painted snuffboxes to serve as models. Quite a few of the Braunschweig snuffboxes have survived in museums. Their flat round lids are bedecked with women's portraits, genre scenes and allegorical paintings. On the inside the lids bear the following inscription in red paint, "Stobwasser's Fabrik in Braunschweig." Petr Korobov never signed his products. Round snuffboxes with engravings pasted underneath a layer of lacquer encountered in many collections are usually ascribed to his factory. Small round engravings were specially made for the needs of applied arts and portrayed *Poor Liza* (the main protagonist of Karamzin's popular short story), *The 1812 Fire of Moscow* and members of the imperial family.

The first trademark appeared on the factory products under Petr Lukutin, Korobov's son-in-law who inherited the factory in 1824. His trademark consisted of the letters "F. P. L." which stood for "Factory Petr Lukutin." From that time and throughout the 19th century until the factory was closed in 1904, the Lukutin family owned the factory. In 1828, Petr Lukutin was conferred the right to stamp his products with the state emblem.

The double-headed Russian eagle thus appeared next to the "F. P. L." initials.

Alongside plain, mass-produced items intended for the public at large and supplied to trade rows or shops, the Lukutin factory also made things to order intended for wealthy merchants and the aristocracy. Executed with rare craftsmanship and delicacy, those products brought fame to Lukutin's artisans in the first half of the 19th century.

Professional miniature painting flourished in Russia in the late 18th and early 19th centuries. Remarkable artists, such as V. L. Borovikovsky, G. I. Skorodumov and E. F. Krendovsky, devoted their skills to it, and several wonderful miniatures were created by well-known draughtsmen and lithographers, among them K. Gampeln, R. K. Zhukovsky and M. M. Zverev. Miniature painting was also on the rise in the applied arts, especially porcelain painting (Gardner's porcelain factory, which was located comparatively not far from Fedoskino, is worth mentioning in this connection), in which genre scenes and pictures of peasant and round dances were in vogue, together with portraits and landscapes. Lukutin's papier-mache lacquer miniatures were well-attuned to their time. Their conventional black background, small size, planar composition, romantic and allegorical scenes or sentimental portraits met perfectly well the aesthetic criteria of the age.

From 1828 Petr Lukutin exhibited his products at industrial and handicraft fairs in Russia and abroad, invariably winning "public acclaim" and the highest awards. His wares were always distinguished by top quality papier-mache and durable lacquer. The boxes and caskets could be quickly and easily sealed with their lids, and often fitted with barely visible hinge joints. Always exquisite and practical, Lukutin's ware of that period displayed diverse decorative designs, in which lacquered papier-mache combined with mosaic miniatures, landscapes painted on enamel or mother-of-pearl inlays.

The splendid brown cigar-case is decorated with a painting after a lithograph *Messenger* by A. O. Orlovsky executed in an original technique — the painting was done in brown against gold leaf. The same technique was used in the painting *Horsemen* emblazoned against the red background of a big tray. In *A View of Ostankino* part of the mother-of-pearl plaque is coated with the finest layers of paint to produce the scumble effect. The artist exploited shimmering mother-of-pearl to depict the shining strips of light in the sky and on the water surface in his landscape. The miniatures *Good News* and *Under an Umbrella* on a snuffbox and a cigar-box of the late 1820s and early 1830s are excellent samples of this superb painting.

A series of items from the 1830s and the 1840s, decorated with the portraits of reigning emperor Nicholas I, were made in a reserved and austere manner. In the snuffbox miniature *Nicholas I Hunting* after F. Kruger's engraving, a mother-of-pearl segment enhances the luminous oil paints and the lacquered black frame creates the impression of a genuinely valuable artifact. Morcelli's miniature, showing the emperor on horseback surrounded by his retinue, was done on paper, placed under a glass in a metal frame and inlaid in the body of the cigar-case. Another snuffbox miniature showing Nicholas I with his wife and son in a boat was also enclosed in a metal frame.

Snuffboxes with sentimental portraits (*Girls with Camomiles* and *A Little Girl with a Kitten*) made in Rococo style date to a later period. These miniatures are surrounded by a rich golden ornament in the shape of fine scrolls done on the surface of the snuffboxes painted in imitation mother-of-pearl.

Lukutin's son, Alexander, who was endowed simultaneously with rare enterprise and refined artistic taste, began to work at the factory in 1843. Under him the craft experienced its heyday, with

Lukutin wares being actively exported and competing successfully on the European market. The Lukutin factory was so popular in Russia that all papier-mache lacquers made at the workshops of the Moscow region came to be called "Lukutin wares."

Rivals to the Korobov-Lukutin factory appeared early in the 19th century. Count Sheremetev's serfs, Yegor and Taras Vishnyakov, opened their workshops in neighbouring Zhostovo and Ostashkovo, respectively, in 1815 and 1816. By the early 1850s, twelve lacquer workshops were operating in Zhostovo and nearby villages. The workshop of Osip Filippovich Vishnyakov soon captured the leading position in the trade. His earlier known works date to the 1830s through the 1850s. They bear the trademark "Master O. F. Vishnyakov" inscribed in a circle. This trademark is found on round snuff-boxes with the picture of an enamoured couple as well as on caskets with architectural landscapes. It should be emphasized that the products of Vishnyakov's workshop are comparatively easily identified and dated because starting from 1865 they bore gold and silver medals won at industrial handicraft fairs as their trademark. The inscription "To Vishnyakov and Sons" signalled that his two sons — Petr and Vassily — had been in business.

In the second half of the 19th century Vishnyakov wares revealed a characteristic peculiarity. There appeared among what were essentially copies of more or less acclaimed originals naive and artless improvisations, mostly rural landscapes, by the Vishnyakov miniaturists. Craftsmen poured out their souls and conveyed sincere feelings in unsophisticated views of small riverside houses with a rosy dawn on the horizon, greatly pleasing to the eye. Vishnyakov masters were especially renowned for their winter landscapes painted on a lacquered black surface dusted with metal powder. They skillfully painted shapely trees and bushes on the prominent surface of their products, with fanciful stumps with branches invariably placed in the foreground and adroitly adding the final touch to their compositions. Those landscapes formed the background to most of Vishnyakov's troikas.

The history of two outstanding lacquer productions in the Moscow region — the Lukutin and Vishnyakov workshops — closely intertwined throughout the 19th century. They competed with and influenced each other, exchanging craftsmen and production techniques.

Lacquer miniatures of the Moscow region were made with the help of multi-layer oil painting on the primed papier-mache surface with special lining. Mother-of-pearl, gold leaf, silver foil and metal powder were broadly used as lining. Painting in translucent layers of paint over various priming and lining was locally referred to as "see-through" as distinct from ordinary thick painting with a "body." It is noteworthy that the Fedoskino technique of combining "see-through" and thick painting, which took shape in the first half of the 19th century, has remained on the whole unchanged up to the present time. Decorative techniques have also survived intact, including "tortoise-shell like" surface painting, *skan'* and guilloching. A design made of tiny silver or German silver spangles inlaid over wet lacquer with another lacquer coating above was called *skan'* in Fedoskino. Designs made by scratching the upper layer of lacquer to the leaf of foil underneath are called guilloching. The "tortoise-shell" effect is produced either with the help of a brush or a candle flame over a red or ochre background. Most of the Fedoskino papier-mache wares have a black background on the outside and are covered inside with scarlet, bright-red or cherry-coloured lacquer.

The technique of monochrome painting on gold leaf was used in a series of mid-19th century Lukutin chinoiseries. Unlike numerous pieces of chinoiseries made in Europe, Lukutin painters invariably strove for three-dimensional representation, enhancing it with shading and at times even relief painting. The painstaking light-and-shade working of gold embellishment with brown colour gave depth to the garlands of grape-vine and oak-tree branches on decorative Easter eggs, which were annually turned out by the Lukutin factory.

Contemporaries did not leave lacquers of the Moscow region, especially those made at the Lukutin and Vishnyakov factories, unnoticed. A report of the All-Russia Agricultural Exhibition held in Kharkov in 1887, stated that: "Products of artisans of the Moscow region are, beyond the shadow of a doubt, foremost among crushed paper and papier-mache wares. Incidentally, Vishnyakov is the major producer of exquisite papier-mache lacquers. These things are called in general Lukutin wares after their top and main producer and sell in huge amounts not only in Russia but also abroad, where they were showcased at numerous international exhibitions and were awarded prizes. Small wonder, if you take into account their perfect workmanship, as well as pictures and vignettes with which they are decorated."

It should be pointed out for the sake of correctness that art critics expressed differing opinions at that time because they applied the same requirements to papier-mache miniatures as they did to easel painting. "Microscopic bric-a-bracs always with faulty pictures and themes so commonplace," was how Vassily Stasov described Moscow lacquers, urging craftsmen to use specimens of a higher quality as models for copying. Contemporaries, however, were fully aware that this verdict was overly harsh. Characterising Lukutin wares as objects of applied arts in his review of the 1886 World Fair in Antwerp, A. A. Efron somewhat simple-heartedly observed, "Peasant scenes and characters are portrayed rather forcefully in every exhibit. Art critics will, unquestionably, find a great deal of drawbacks and errors in every painting, but for the public buying these inexpensive table decorations, they are artistic enough."

Papier-mache lacquers of the Moscow region were closely linked to Russia's graphic art of that period. Miniature artists mastered and copied drawings, engravings, cheap folk prints and lithographs which were sold in separate sheets and albums. Quite a few works have now been identified as prototypes of miniature compositions used in lacquers of the Moscow region.

Many popular 19th century illustrated periodicals, in particular the *Russky Khudozhestvenny Listok* (Russian Art Gazette), published by V. Timm in the 1850s and the 1860s, often suggested compositions to local artists. Thus, issue No. 29 of 1857 carried a reproduction of A. A. Popov's painting *Demian's Fish Soup*. The lithograph was accompanied by a text reading that the author was awarded a gold medal at the Academy of Arts' exhibition and that the original painting belonged to the Emperor. "The publisher received the original painting from the palace on His Majesty's consent and hoped to satisfy the desire of those who had been unable to enjoy it at the exhibition to see this picture reproduced here." Timm's text must have served as good advertising, and the owners of lacquer workshops and the Lukutin factory hoped that their wares sporting that picture would be a success. The original composition was generalised to the utmost extent in miniatures, with minimum details left — a set table, a bit of the interior and a window. In some miniatures the interior is fully replaced by the black background or a landscape next to a peasant hut. Three figures are clearly outlined against the black background. Silverish colour spots woven rhythmically into the clothes and parts of the interior make the composition particularly expressive.

In the 1860s V. Timm often published I. I. Sokolov's drawings dealing with Ukrainian peasant life, a theme which was extremely popular after the smashing success of Gogol's *Ukrainian Tales*. Artists of the Moscow region made use of some of Sokolov's works. Thus, the *Ukrainian Woman* theme borrowed from a lithograph published by the *Russky Listok* is often encountered in Fedoskino miniatures.

A miniature on the lid of a blotting-case made in the Vishnyakov's workshop in the 1870s is a rare example of a nearly exact life-size copy of that drawing. The miniature was executed scrupulously, with all the details of the landscape faithfully reproduced. The thin layers of paints laid over the silverish background convey a mysterious shimmering atmosphere. The colour pattern is tactful and austere: the bright spots of the young girl's skirt and the garland stand out against the general golden ochre background. The serene and well-balanced composition on the blotting-case differs from Sokolov's drawing with its jocular content. The miniature fully meets the purpose of embellishing an expensive and stylish writing-desk accessory.

The same theme in a largely modified version showing *A Ukrainian Woman with a Yoke* is often encountered in museum collections. The young girl is depicted by a riverside on the outskirts of a village against a light silverish landscape in the background. This delicate landscape creates a naively pure image, whose lyricism is akin to the generalising symbols redolent of folk art.

R. K. Zhukovsky's lithograph *Returning from a Fair* from the *Russian Folk Scenes* album has undergone a fascinating transformation. The amusing scene shows three inebriated men riding in a cart and singing a song, whose lyrics are, apparently, given below the picture, "Once upon a time there were these men, saffron milk-cap mushrooms're growing...." Though original works were nearly copied verbatim in some Lukutin wares, more specimens survived with modified compositions. There are, for example, three drunk men (whose figures are exact copies of Zhukovsky's lithograph) in the company of the fourth man, sitting at an inn table (instead of in a cart) with a bottle and some snacks.

The theme of troika-riding was most widespread in 19th century miniatures of the Moscow region. Engravings by A. Orlovsky and K. Gampeln are known to have served as sources for "summer troika" miniatures. The lithograph *Emperor Alexander Nikolayevich and Empress Maria Alexandrovna* from V. Timm's aforementioned publication was used to paint numerous "winter troika" compositions. The lithograph shows the imperial couple riding in a sledge through wintry St. Petersburg. The Empress has an expressive *bavolet* headdress with wide ribbons tied in a bow as was fashionable in the 1860s. There is a casket with an exact copy of this lithograph at the State History Museum. Significantly modified versions were, however, far more widespread. Evidently every craftsman chose a composition to his liking, adding at will a landscape, which was a figment of his imagination. A troika rushing through the snow-laden forest and sledge riders, rosy-cheeked with the frost and sporting bright costumes, all scarcely resembled the austere monochrome engraving with the imperial couple, decorously riding through Senate Square. By creatively interpreting V. Timm's drawings, Fedoskino painters produced fundamentally different miniatures, which were destined to survive in the local craft for over a century. These pictures of "winter" and "summer" troikas are to this day a popular theme that has become an emblem of the craft.

The range of papier-mache products of the Lukutin factory and the Vishnyakovs' workshops was very wide and intended for the public at large. Small items, such as pocket and table matchboxes, cigar cases, sets of travelling cups, tea-caddies, tobacco boxes, purses, caskets and cases of most diverse shapes and uses, were part of the people's household, serving to decorate a writing-desk, a dressing-table or often as a desirable gift. This fact is graphically illustrated by numerous extant inscriptions, including "In memory from Ivan Pitrovich Tomos 1873" or "To Pavel from Maria 25 December, 1892".

Paper lacquer factories produced larger pieces, such as photograph albums and shelves, blotting-cases, tables and all sorts of trays, with the latter often used as pieces of interior decoration. Such "pictures" of landscapes, bouquets of flowers, still lifes and genre scenes were given a prominent place or graced the walls of provincial hotels, inns, shops and taverns. Few papier-mache trays have survived. Their fragility prompted craftsmen to turn to a more lasting material. In the mid-19th century Vishnyakov's workshop launched the production of metal trays. Miniature artists were equally skilled at painting papier-mache and metal plates, biscuit dishes and trays. Both productions involved many similar techniques, such as filling, lacquering and polishing. The production, of painted metal trays, subsequently, branched into a separate industry — the famous Zhostovo trays.

Throughout the 19th century Fedoskino miniatures were closely connected with professional art, reacting to the change of styles and fashions. Fedoskino painting developed parallel to miniature painting in other areas of the applied arts. By the late 19th century photography had become widespread, leading to the decline of miniature painting. The laws of miniature painting with its closed space and conventional fantastic lighting were at variance with the latest achievements of *plein air* painting. The refined Art Nouveau style that came into vogue in professional applied art, especially porcelain painting, could hardly find acceptance among peasant artists.

In 1904, Lukutin's heirs (the last, N. A. Lukutin died in 1902) closed the factory. Some miniature painters transferred to the Vishnyakov workshop, but many of them were dissatisfied with the tough working conditions. The Fedoskino Artel of Former Lukutin Factory Workers was founded in 1910, initially numbering ten craftsmen, later joined by several more people. Financial support rendered to the new artel by the gubernia authorities and the handicraft curator S. T. Morozov played an important role in maintaining the Fedoskino craft alive during those years. The Moscow Handicrafts Museum, which developed new copying models, also promoted

its creativity. Silhouette compositions with black lacquer pictures against a yellow or bronze-powder background proved most successful. Genre scenes, pictures of farm work or architectural landscapes were the dominant themes. The artel's products were displayed at the All-Russia Exhibition of Agriculture in Kiev in 1913 and won a small gold medal, whose picture began to be stamped on the back side of products next to the name of the artel.

The years of the revolution and the subsequent Civil War took a heavy toll on the craftsmen and, for that matter, Russian life in general. Workshops often stood idle as a result of raw material and other shortages, and there was little demand for the finished products. The new gubernia authorities frowned upon artisans producing "bourgeois" goods. Any time at all craftsmen could be branded as "kulaks" and private owners, with all the ensuing repercussions. That situation changed noticeably in 1923, when the All-Union Exhibition of Agricultural, Industrial and Cultural Products was held in Moscow, where Fedoskino wares were awarded the first degree diploma "for superb artistic skill" and another diploma "for preserving the craft and high cooperation." Artel's products were exported abroad and sent to international exhibitions. Fedoskino craftsmen were awarded the Paris Exhibition diploma in 1925 and the Milan Exhibition diploma in 1927.

In 1928, a group of especially gifted painters from among the Vishnyakov miniaturists joined the artel. Their skill, especially in making landscapes, tangibly enriched the Fedoskino craft. The artel's artists managed to perpetuate traditional craftsmanship and pass their skills on to the younger generation. This cause was largely promoted by the opening of a miniature painting vocational school at Fedoskino in 1931.

Important anniversaries of Soviet political and cultural life, which brought major state orders, became landmarks in the craft's history. Thus, a major exhibition held in 1937 marked the centenary of Pushkin's death. A special series of caskets centered around Pushkinian themes, with paintings by D. N. Kardovsky, G. G. Chernetsov and G. D. Myasoyedov portraying Pushkin or illustrating his works used as models. The miniatures were accomplished by gifted artists from among the early graduates of the Fedoskino school, including I. Bannov, K. Zorin, S. Slesarev and N. Smurov, who brilliantly succeeded in copying academic painting. Many of them, regrettably, were not destined to work long: they perished during World War II.

Throughout the 1940s and 1950s the artel focused primarily on copying works by Vassily Perov, Vassily Surikov, Ilya Repin, Ivan Shishkin and other renowned Russian artists. Some pieces, such as Vasnetsov's *Alenushka* were easily transposed onto the surface of caskets. However, as few easel paintings could be adapted to the laws of miniature painting, the more creative artists came up with their own compositions. During that period V. D. Lipitsky, A. I. Kozlov and M. G. Pashinin emerged as original artists, who turned to Russian tales, such as *The Scarlet Flower*, *The Tale of Tsar Saltan* and *The Snow Maiden*, which was a new trend for the Fedoskino craft. Ever since that time Russian tales became a popular theme among Fedoskino artists, whose poetic images have lost none of their glamour.

M. S. Chizhov was an outstanding Fedoskino artist and chronicler. Old decoration techniques have been restored by contemporary Fedoskino artists in large measure owing to his works. He developed his own school of miniature painting, as exemplified by his *Winter in Fedoskino*, which gives a panoramic view of the village and shows traditional winter fetes. Chizhov's miniatures have embodied the best artistic heritage and serve as a graphic example of Fedoskino craft of the Soviet period.

Landscape miniatures gained prominence in the sixties. Using the decorative potential of painting over metal (bronze or aluminum) powder, I. I. Strakhov produced series of memorable landscapes, including winter landscapes with silvery snow, spring landscapes with a radiant sky at sunset and autumn landscapes with golden leaves. S. P. Rogatov managed to cast off the influence of easel painting in his luxurious lyrical landscapes. His views of Fedoskino and the nearby villages of Kryukovo and Semenishchevo were in keeping with the laws of early 19th century landscape painting, with the composition hinging on the planar principle.

The work of Y. V. Karapayev marked a fundamentally new stage in the development of landscape painting. His scumbling on a gold or mother-of-pearl surface combined with airy drawing revealed for many Fedoskino craftsmen the enchanting radiance of landscape miniatures. This genre flourished in the 1980s and is now going strong in works by G. I. Larishev, G. V. Skripunov, Y. L. Dubovikov and Y. S. Shishkin. The artists deftly transform shimmering mother-of-pearl into glimmering water, sky at sunset or sunbeams piercing clouds.

Works by Alexander Fedorov are also praiseworthy. Art aficionados are attracted by his workmanship, the tiny dimensions of his miniatures, their high-relief framing, immaculate polishing and his ever-present gold filigree trademark monogram. Fedorov has renounced the traditional black background for a dark brown palette, which suits better the warm colours of his landscapes.

Portraiture is the most complicated and demanding genre of miniature painting. Many Fedoskino painters show a perfect command of the copying technique, are skilled at making miniature portraits to order by photographs and enjoy copying well-known miniatures of the first half of the 19th century. Portraits of female pulchritude from Pushkin's time, such as Countess Volkonskaya and Pushkin's wife Natalia Goncharova, are especially popular. Few craftsmen, however, are capable of creating original works of their own. Thus, M. S. Chizhov produced in the 1960s a series of portraits of his teachers — veteran Fedoskino miniaturists V. D. Lipitsky and M. G. Pashinin, who for several decades portrayed famous Russian and Soviet politicians, scientists and cultural figures.

In the 1960s and throughout the 1980s, the Fedoskino factory put out boxes and caskets with Russian-style salon scenes, most of which were exported. Another group of Fedoskino wares consisted of caskets and panels with pompous multi-figure compositions, which were intended as rich and prestigious gifts more often than not from one organization to another. State orders allowed the painters to remove themselves from marketing problems thereby doing little to enhance creative quests. The utilitarian value of products receded to the background and their shape culture was largely lost.

Serious changes occurred in the ideological orientation of Russian society in the late 1980s. Restrictions, which formerly curbed creative freedom and prevented artists from self-expression, were lifted. Interest surged in the Russian cultural heritage and especially the decorative and applied arts, giving rise to a new market for unique and expensive artifacts.

New trends found favorable ground in Fedoskino, largely prepared by G. I. Larishev, People's Artist of Russia. As an instructor of an entire generation of Fedoskino craftsmen he managed to expand the pictorial potentialities of miniatures, awakening creative powers among young artists. Enriched by novel artistic methods, their craft has stuck to the mainstream of the local tradition. In conformity with the tastes of the first half of the 19th century boxes and caskets are again treated not merely as pieces of miniature painting but above all as genuine works of art in which shape, colour scheme and decor are on an even par with painting. Despite their delicacy and seeming fragility, papier-mache products are expected to remain convenient, durable and functionable. Lacquer works by A. I. Kuznetsov,

N. A. Zotov and A. A. Moshchevitin beckon to be touched and handled: there is something alive lurking in their prominent flowing shapes, rounded corners, shafts at the base and refined ball-shaped legs. Romantic landscapes or reserved ornaments in a noble colour scheme never dominate but are always subordinate to the shape conceived by the artist.

A different relationship between painting and product typifies lacquer works by Sergei and Alla Kozlovs, who lay emphasis on a chosen theme. The shape and decor are only meant to underscore the impression produced by the miniature. An airy monochrome view of Marfino emerges in a haze on an exquisite black-lacquer box like a vision of bygone centuries. Another box is decorated with a winter panorama of the Trinity-Sergius Monastery. A delightful design envelopes the entire surface of the box as if it were some precious silvery lace and creates a wonderfully poetic picture of the monastery, whose handsome architecture is enchanting at any time of the year. Shape is in perfect harmony with painting in a series of shallow-bottomed cases with high original lids shaped as painted onion-domes which traditionally crown Russian towers and churches.

Many contemporary Fedoskino painters experiment with form. Thus, Dmitri Rogatov created a fascinating tall rectangular case for a perfume flask, elaborating the theme of the time of Empress Elizabeth under the impression of his visit to parks in the environs of St. Petersburg. The lid and all sides of the case bear depictions, forming an integral pictorial space showing an ivy-grown summerhouse, in which a lady-in-waiting is hiding with her cavalier. There is another original piece by Vladimir Rogatov — a vertical cylindrical box with a lid in the shape of a snow-white rotunda. Elegant, whimsically shaped boxes by N. V. Strelkina (Burbysheva), I. A. Isayev and A. I. Kuznetsov are no less eye-catching.

The idea of a "living" papier-mache product, in which painting and the object itself form an integral whole is taken to the extreme in the works of A. V. Korchagin. A graphic example is his work *Dedicated to Gogol*, a tiny chest of drawers or travelling casket with a lot of compartments and small drawers. On the inside and the outside it is covered with finest grisaille-style paintings in brown shades showing scenes from lives of Gogol's characters.

N. M. Soloninkin was quite a success in miniature portraits. His virtuoso technique, perfect knowledge of numerous works of the past centuries and reliance on old painting and graphic stylistic features has enabled Soloninkin to execute original works of art with his distinctive, often romantic treatment of his personages. His portraits of members of the Romanov Dynasty, revealing the Baroque tradition and the same colour scheme, is indicative in this respect.

Traditional Fedoskino ornamentation of boxes reached extraordinary heights in the 1980s and 1990s. Today's Fedoskino *skan'* is incomparably richer than Lukutin's artless designs. Using a limited set of figured metal spangles - tiny circles, corners, crescents and stars - latterday craftsmen create an unlimited number of ornaments inscribed on the round or oval lid of a box, girdling its prominent sides or just framing paintings. One of Fedoskino veteran masters, Sergei Monashov, is unsurpassed in the skill of *skan'*-making. Gold and silver spangles alternate rhythmically throughout the black, blue or red surface of his lacquer boxes. His ornaments echo patterns of snakeskin, fish scales, peacock feathers or Russian hauberk intertwined in most intricate ways. Younger painters, too, are mastering this exceedingly painstaking technique. Moshchevitin, Isayev and A. Fedorov use *skan'* to frame their miniatures, making their pieces especially expressive and decorative.

Fedoskino painters also continue to develop genre miniatures. They have shown far more freedom in recent years in elaborating a multitude of themes. Unrestrained in conveying their feelings and ideas, they turn out hearty works of art. Historical and ethnographic themes are being extensively added to traditional fairy tale, epic song motifs and illustrations of literary works.

Nadezhda Strelkina (Burbysheva) evinces keen interest in old Russian costume in her lacquers. Her "see-through" painting on gold leaf captures the beauty of gold-embroidered *boyar* attire. Mrs. Strelkina must have inherited the knack of using gold and silver, which look prominent and simultaneously delicate: at the turn of the century her great-grandfather ran a lacquer workshop at Zhostovo and was famous for his painted silver cigar-boxes and goblets. Moscow merchant costume and scenes of the merchant lifestyle can be seen in the box *An Apprentice* by I. V. Kombarova and in another piece titled *A Fabric Shop* by Isayev. Fedoskino painters feel a special kinship with patriarchal Russian culture and consistantly portray traditional scenes, such as feasting, trysts on the village outskirts and Shrovetide reveling. These scenes are masterfully depicted in M. and S. Rogatovs's box and cigar-case, as well as in brooches produced by S. P. Marchukova (jeweller A. G. Golikov).

Vladimir Rogatov's gorgeous big casket shows the building of St. Petersburg. Inside on a detachable shelf are four smaller boxes decorated with scenes illustrating Peter the Great's reforms of the *boyar* way of life to match European lifestyle. Interpreted in a humorous folklore manner, these scenes are very amusing. Every box is decorated with the same "tortoise-shell smoking" and bears a golden St. Andrew's cross along with a double-headed eagle.

Valery Kovalev reveals limitless imagination in painting sundry horse-drawn wagons, including countless variations of traditional flying "summer" and "winter" troikas and his distinctive well-balanced compositions. In his winter forest cycle Fedoskino's usual black-lacquer background is exceptionally justified in depicting the nocturnal sky, clear and frosty, which is set against fancifully decorative white snow-covered trees, mysterious-looking huge heaps of snow and wondrous light illuminating a solitary carriage driven by a tired horse. This compelling scene makes the viewer sympathize with travellers stranded in the forest at night.

Vladimir Domakhin draws on Vishnyakov's primitivist naive pictorial tradition in his reserved works. After studying the principles of Zhostovo miniature painting and those of Russian *lubok* (folk prints) in general, Domakhin paints reminiscences from 19th century life, stylizing his miniatures in imitation of old Vishnyakov masters and savouring the pointedly conventional representation of space, stage-like lighting and even typical "Vishnyakov" details, such as the indispensable tree stump in the foreground. Obviously, the muted brownish colour scheme should also call to mind the faded varnish of old miniatures. The artist is fond of the old masters and find nothing wrong with imitating them.

It is not so easy to squeeze modern life into the realm of miniature painting. Nonetheless, some artists see enough alluring forms and poetry around to meet the requirements of miniature painting. S. S. Chistov and N. G. Marchukov focus on the elements of contemporary life. V. D. Antonov and E. Y. Khomutinnikova turn to the moving image of a young mother with child as an eternal symbol of new life.

The Fedoskino art school stores a collection of 19th century lacquer miniatures as well as diploma works of its graduates from the 1930s onwards. A close acquaintance with this collection is inalienable from the process of training young Fedoskino craftsmen, who are thus assimilating their artistic heritage. Two kilometers away from Fedoskino is the Marfino estate, a splendid architectural monument dating from the first half of the 19th century, whose image is just as frequently encountered in both old and modern Fedoskino works. Artists never tear of admiring the picturesque environs of their native village and the view of the newly restored wooden church of St. Nicholas the Wonder-worker on the high Ucha bank. Opposite the present-day factory still stands the old building of former Lukutin's workshops, where the great-grandfathers of today's masters painstakingly turned out exquisite papier-mache lacquers.

The immutable charm of the native land and continuity of the craft, which earns the artisans their daily bread and sense of achievement, account for the longevity of Fedoskino lacquers.

Illustrations

1. *Restaurant Scene* snuffbox
P. I. Korobov Factory, early 19th century

2. Snuffbox with a portrait of the Grand Duke Constantin Pavlovich
P. I. Korobov Factory, early 19th century

3. *Poor Liza* snuffbox
P. I. Korobov Factory, early 19th century

4. *Cleopatra* snuffbox
J. H. Stobwasser Factory, Germany, early 19th century

5. *Modest Young Girl* snuffbox
P. I. Korobov Factory, early 19th century

6. *Angelica* snuffbox
P. V. Lukutin Factory, the 1820s

7. *Lady in Turban* snuffbox
P. V. Lukutin Factory, the 1830s

8. A. O. Orlovsky
Messenger lithograph, 1821

9. *Messenger* cigar-case
P. V. Lukutin Factory, 1825-1828

10. *Summer Troika* cigar-case
P. V. and A. P. Lukutins Factory, the 1840s

11. *Horsemen* tray. After A. O. Orlovsky
P. V. Lukutin Factory, the 1830s

12, 13. Set of travelling cups and a cigar-case
P. V. Lukutin Factory, the 1820s-1830s

14-18. *Good News* snuffbox
P. V. Lukutin Factory, the 1830s

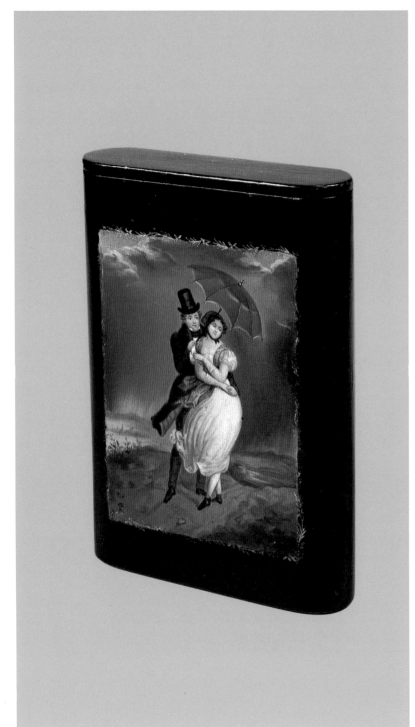

19. *Under an Umbrella* cigar-case
P. V. Lukutin Factory, the 1820s

20. *Lake in the Mountains* snuffbox
P. V. Lukutin Factory, the 1820s

21. *Count D. N. Sheremetev's Village of Ostankino* snuffbox
P. V. Lukutin Factory, the 1830s

22. *Catherine* snuffbox
A. P. Lukutin Factory, the 1860s

23. Snuffbox with a woman's portrait
O. F. Vishnyakov Workshop, the 1840s

27

24. *Landscape with Fishermen* snuffbox
O. F. Vishnyakov Workshop, the 1840s

25. *A Lady with a Cavalier* snuffbox
O. F. Vishnyakov Workshop, the 1840s

26. *Boys Feeding Puppies* cigar-case with matchbox
O. F. Vishnyakov Workshop, the 1860s

27. *Emperor Nicholas I, Grand Duke Mikhail Pavlovich, Tsesarevich Alexander Nikolayevich, Prince P. M. Volkonsky and Count A. K. Benkendorf* cigar-case
G. Morcelli after an original by F. Kruger
P. V. Lukutin Factory, the 1830s

28. *Emperor Nicholas I Hunting* snuffbox
P. V. Lukutin Factory, the 1830s

29. *Emperor Nicholas I and Empress Alexandra Fedorovna with Their Son* snuffbox
P. V. Lukutin Factory, the 1830s

29

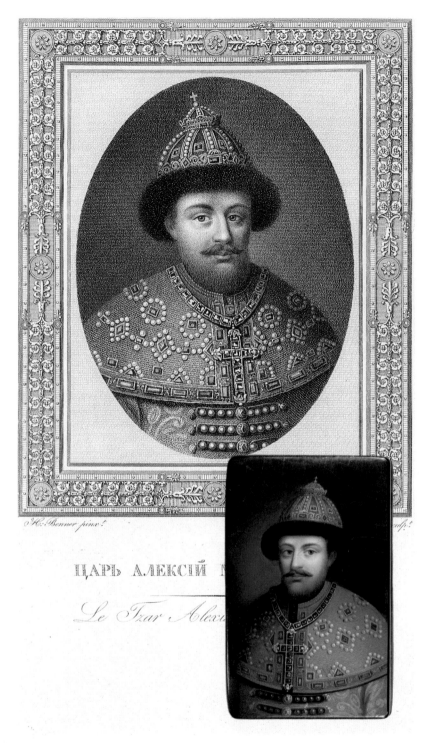

30

30. Engraving with a Portrait of Tsar Alexei Mikhailovich, 1817
After an original by A. Benner

32. Engraving with a Portrait of Alexander I, 1817
After an original by A. Benner

31. Snuffbox with a Portrait of Tsar Alexei Mikhailovich
P. V. and A. P. Lukutins Factory, the 1850s

33. Snuffbox with a Portrait of Alexander I
P. V. and A. P. Lukutins Factory, the 1850s

34. Engraving with a Portrait of Tsarevna Sofia, 1817
After an original by A. Benner

36. Snuffbox with a Portrait of Count M. S. Vorontsov
P. V. and A. P. Lukutins Factory, the 1850s

35. Snuffbox with a Portrait of Tsarevna Sofia
P. V. and A. P. Lukutins Factory, the 1850s

37. *Homer with the Muse* snuffbox
P. V. and A. P. Lukutins Factory, the 1850s

38. *Young Girl in Yellow* snuffbox
P. V. and A. P. Lukutins Factory, the 1850s

39. *Artist's Family* snuffbox
P. V. and A. P. Lukutins Factory, the 1840s

40. *Berta and Serafina* snuffbox
P. V. and A. P. Lukutins Factory, the 1840s

41. *Young Girl with a Kitten* snuffbox
P. V. and A. P. Lukutins Factory, the 1840s

42. Snuffbox
P. V. and A. P. Lukutins Factory, the 1840s

43. Snuffbox with Chinoiserie
P. V. and A. P. Lukutins Factory, the 1840s

44. *Girls with Camomiles* snuffbox
P. V. and A. P. Lukutins Factory, the 1850s

45. *Listening to a Song* box
P. V. and A. P. Lukutins Factory, the 1850s

46. *Wreath* snuffbox
P. V. and A. P. Lukutins Factory, the 1850s

47. *Bird in a Cage* snuffbox
A. P. Lukutin Factory, the 1860s

48. *Young Girl with a Book* cigar-case
P. V. and A. P. Lukutins Factory, the 1850s

49. *Would You Like a Drink?* cigarette-case
P. V. and A. P. Lukutins Factory, the 1850s

50. *Dance* album
Workshop of the Vishnyakovs's Circle, the 1880s

51-62. Lukutins' Factory products,
the 1830s-1870s

63. V. F. Timm
Emperor Alexander Nikolayevich and Empress Maria Alexandrovna, lithograph, 1858

64. *Emperor Alexander II and the Empress in a Sledge* box
A. P. Lukutin Factory, the 1860s

65-69. V. O. Vishnyakov Workshop products, the 1880s, and those
of I. P. Vishnyakov Workshop, 1890s

70. *A Ukrainian Woman*,
lithograph, 1861
After a drawing by I. I. Sokolov

71. *A Ukrainian Woman*
with a Yoke matchbox
A. P. Lukutin Factory, the 1860s

72. *A Ukrainian Woman*
with a Yoke box
V. O. Vishnyakov Workshop,
the 1880s

73. *A Ukrainian Woman* blotting-case
O. F. Vishnyakov Workshop, the 1870s

74. R. K. Zhukovsky
Returning from a Fair, lithograph,
1841

75. *Returning from a Fair* box
A. P. Lukutin Factory, the 1860s

76. *Merry-Making* album
A. P. Lukutin Factory, the 1870s

77. *Merry-Making* snuffbox
O. F. Vishnyakov Workshop, the 1860s

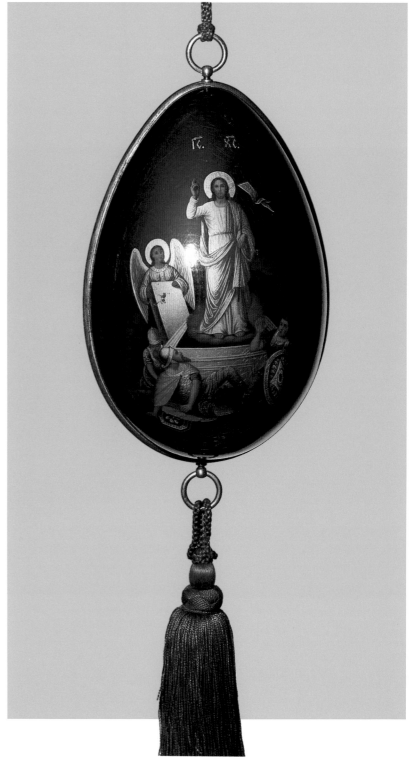

78. Easter Egg
N. A. Lukutin Factory, the 1890s

79-81. *Trinity* icon. N. A. Lukutin Factory, the 1900s
Easter Eggs. A. P. Lukutin Factory, 1866 and 1867

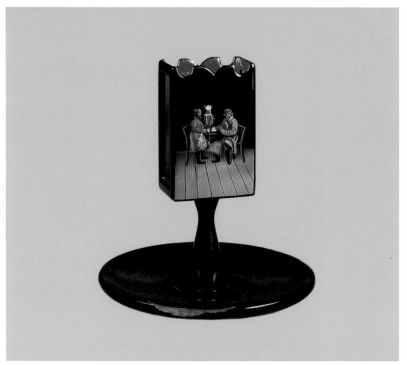

82. *Tea-drinking* matchbox
V. O. Vishnyakov Workshop, the 1880s

83. *Tea-drinking* keg
A. P. Lukutin Factory, the 1860s

84. *Tea-drinking* snuffbox
A. P. Lukutin Factory, the 1860s

85. *Tryst by a Hut* purse. After a drawing by K. A. Trutovsky
A. P. Lukutin Factory, the 1880s

86. *Demian's Fish Soup* cigarette-case
V. O. Vishnyakov Workshop, the 1870s

87. P.-M. Roussel
A Happy Family, lithograph,
1840

88. *A Happy Family* keg
A. P. Lukutin Factory,
the 1860s

89. *Drum* box
O. F. Vishnyakov Workshop, the 1880s

90. *Malachite* tea-caddy
V. O. Vishnyakov Workshop, the 1890s

91. *Dance* keg
Unknown Workshop of the Vishnyakovs' Circle, the 1890s

92. *Round Dance* plate
O. F. Vishnyakov Workshop, the 1880s

93. *Abduction* keg
P. O. Vishnyakov Workshop, the 1880s

94. *Winter Troika* casket
O. F. Vishnyakov Workshop, the 1880s

95. *Hunter* keg
V. O. Vishnyakov Workshop, the 1880s

96. *Snow-storm* powder-box
A. P. and N. A. Lukutins Factory, the 1880s

97. *Riverside House* snuffbox
V. O. Vishnyakov Workshop, the 1880s

98. *Landscape with a Bridge* snuffbox
V. O. Vishnyakov Workshop, the 1880s

99. Card-case
O. F. Vishnyakov Workshop, the 1880s

100-112. Vishnyakovs' Workshop products,
the 1860s-1890s

113. *Summer Troika* box
O. F. Vishnyakov Workshop, the 1870s

114. S. G. Platonov
Winter Sledges album plate, the 1880s

115. *Mummers with a Bear* casket
V. O. Vishnyakov Workshop, the 1890s

116. *Winter Night* biscuit dish
V. O. Vishnyakov Workshop, the 1890s

117. *Winter Troika* cigar-case
Burbyshevs' Workshop, after 1910

118. *Summer Holiday in Ukraine* box
Novoseltsevo Village Workshop, the 1880s

119. *After Mowing* biscuit dish
N. A. Lukutin Factory, the 1890s

120. *Damsel by a Hedge* box. After an original by K. E. Makovsky
N. A. Lukutin Factory, the 1890s

121. *Young Girls Telling Fortune by Wreaths* box
N. A. Lukutin Factory, the 1890s

122. *Attacking Wolves* box
Fedoskino Artel, the 1930s

123. Box with a silhouette picture
Fedoskino Artel of Former Lukutin Factory Masters, after 1910

124. N. S. Semenov
Shepherd box, the 1930s

125. M. K. Papenov
To a Fair box, 1946

126. I. I. Bannov
Station-master plate, 1937

127. K. I. Zorin
Pushkin among the Decembrists box, 1937. After an original by D. N. Kardovsky

128. M. S. Chizhov
Lay of Igor's Host casket, 1950

129. V. N. Samsonov
Bayan Poet box, 1950

130. M. S. Chizhov
Harvest-woman box, 1950

131. M. G. Pashinin
Russian Dance case, 1957

132. Y. V. Gusev
Evenings Outside Moscow casket, 1958

133. M. S. Chizhov
Liberation of Volokolamsk box, 1966

134. M. S. Chizhov
Fedoskino. Winter casket, 1968

135. I. I. Strakhov
Landscape with a Bridge casket, 1957

136. I. I. Strakhov
Landscape with a Cabin box, 1969

137. S. P. Rogatov
After Rain box, 1989

138. L. A. Stroganova
After Reaping box, 1989

139. S. S. Rogatov
Autumn box, 1988

140. S. P. Rogatov
Landscape. Fedoskino casket, 1990

141. V. D. Lipitsky
Night in the Village casket, 1979

142. M. G. Pashinin
Pushkin Visiting Gogol box, 1981

143. V. I. Tretyakov
Great Russians casket, 1994. After an original by H.-F. C. Pauli

144. M. G. Pashinin
Pushkin on the Neva box, 1956

145. M. I. Kornienko
Church of the Intercession on the Nerl box, 1987

146. N. V. Strelkina (Burbysheva)
Scarlet Flower box, 1990

147. V. I. Tretyakov
On a Walk case, 1994

148-150. G. V. Skripunov
Kirill-Belozersky Monastery casket, 1991. *Russian Winter*, 1994, and *Early Snow*, 1993, boxes

151. Y. S. Shishkin
Winter Night. Fedoskino casket, 1993

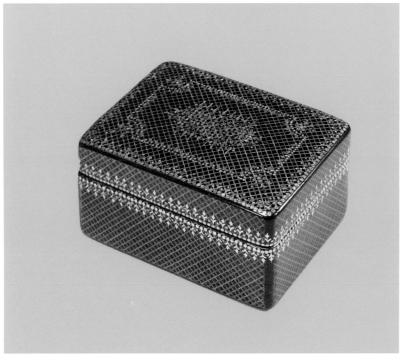

152. S. V. Monashov
Festive box, 1992

153, 154. S. V. Monashov
Peacock Feather keg, 1989. Oval case, 1993

155. Y. V. Gusev
Blue Wave box, 1983

156. V. O. Kalinin
Still Life box, 1992

157. N. G. Marchukov
Pskov Kremlin box, 1994

158. S. P. Marchukova, A. G. Golikov (jeweller)
Winter Troika brooch, 1993

159. S. P. Marchukova, A. G. Golikov (jeweller)
Summer Troika brooch, 1993

160. L. N. Krasnoslobodtseva
Little Khavroshechka box, 1994

161. N. M. Soloninkin
Casket with a Portrait of Mikhail Lomonosov, 1991

162-165. N. M. Soloninkin, B. N. Korneyev (jeweller)
Medallions with the Portraits: Tsar Mikhail Fedorovich, Empress Catherine II, Emperor Nicholas I, Emperor Alexander III, 1995

166. P. N. Puchkov
Evening Bells (Trinity-Sergius Lavra) casket, 1991

„Вечерный звон“

167. V. D. Antonov
Fedoskino Landscapes casket, 1994

168. V. V. Rogatov
The Great Reformer set of caskets, 1994

169. D. V. Rogatov
Tryst in a Summer House case, 1995

170. N. V. Strelkina (Burbysheva)
Day and Night box, 1994

171. N. V. Strelkina (Burbysheva)
Pretty Lasses box, 1994

172. V. V. Rogatov
In an Old Park box, 1995

173. A. V. Korchagin
Dedicated to Gogol triptych (boxes *Great-coat*, *Dead Souls* and *The Nose*), 1995

174-180. A. A. Moshchevitin
Grandfather Yegor, 1991; *August*, 1983; *Backwater*, 1992; *Evening*, 1992, caskets

Y. A. Moshchevitina
Flowers casket, 1992

A. A. Fedorov
Autumn Coming, 1993; *Signs of Spring*, 1992, boxes

181. Y. V. Karapayev
Darling casket, 1994

182. A. A. Kozlova
Case, 1992

183. L. S. Rogatova
By the Well case, 1994

184. Y. V. Karapayev
Tryst box, 1980

185. S. I. Kozlov
Alexander Pushkin and Natalia Goncharova casket, 1993

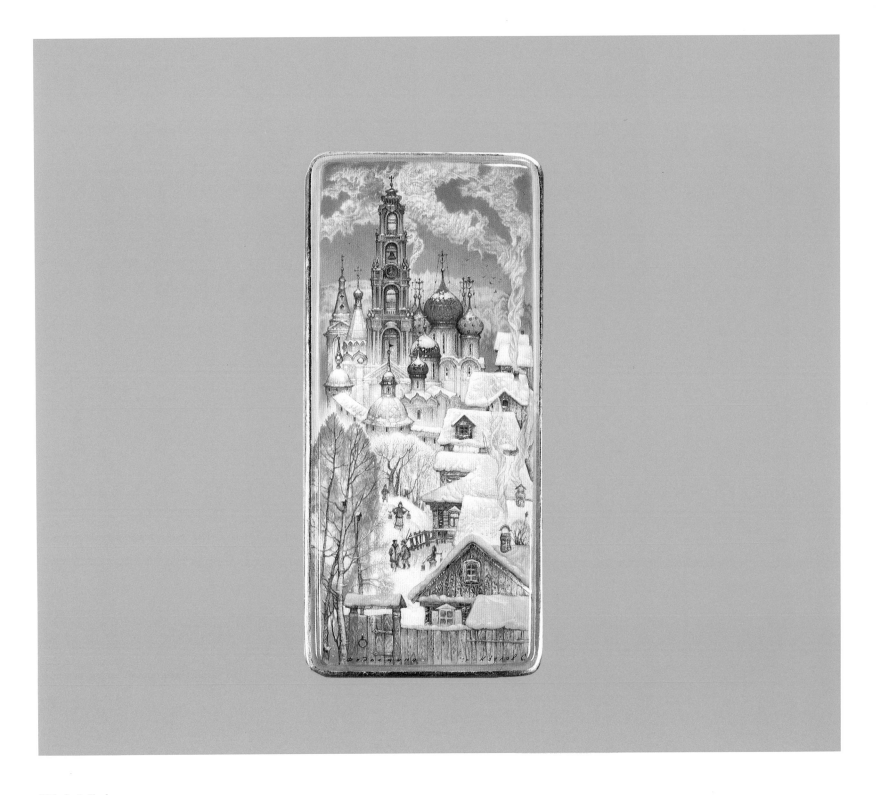

186. S. I. Kozlov
Winter at Sergiev Posad casket, 1994

187. Y. V. Karapayev
April casket, 1984

100

188. G. I. Larishev
Halloo, Halloo, Annushka casket, 1991

189-195. O. I. Shapkin
Dream box, 1995
Pushkin and Gypsies case, 1994

S. S. Rogatov
St. Basil's Cathedral casket, 1994

N. A. Zotov
Winter tea-caddy, 1988

V. V. Sinelnikova (Kuzmenko)
At the Skating-Rink casket, 1994

M. A. Tugarinov
Marfino casket, 1991

V. S. Kovalev
Winter Troika casket, 1993

196. S. S. Chistov
Yemelya casket, 1993

197. V. S. Kovalev
Night box, 1994

198. I. A. Isayev
Tea-drinking case, 1992

199. N. A. Zotov
Bird Cherry box, 1993

200. V. N. Domakhin
Water-carrier casket, 1990

201. V. N. Domakhin
Bad News casket, 1994

202. S. S. Rogatov
Night in the Village box, 1994

203. M. S. Rogatova
At a Tea-House casket, 1993

204. V. V. Sinelnikova (Kuzmenko)
A Couple box, 1994

205. Y. Y. Khomutinnikova
Morning box, 1994

206. V. S. Kovalev
Wedding casket, 1993

207. I. A. Isayev
At a Fabric Shop box, 1993

208. M. S. Wagner
Meeting a Guest box, 1990

209. N. A. Zotov
Tsarevna the Frog casket, 1989

210. V. N. Domakhin
Peasant Wedding casket, 1990

211. V. V. Sinelnikova (Kuzmenko)
Marfino case, 1993

212. S. I. Kozlov
Marfino casket, 1987

213. V. S. Kovalev
Winter Troikas casket, 1992

214. I. V. Kombarova
An Apprentice box, 1994

215. V. D. Antonov
Indian Summer casket, 1994

112

216. D. V. Rogatov
Russian Icarus casket, 1991

217. M. I. Kornienko
Fedoskino Landscape at Night box, 1994

218. A. A. Tolstov
Winter box, 1981

219. A. A. Fedorov
An Old Bridge casket, 1988

220. A. A. Fedorov
In the Woods casket, 1987

221-223. Y. V. Gusev
Caskets, 1988 and 1984. Case, 1987

224. A. A. Moshchevitin
Winter Forest decorative panel, 1993

Makers' Marks on Fedoskino Products
of the 19th through the 20th Century

P. V. Lukutin Factory, 1818-1828

P. V. Lukutin Factory, 1828-1843

P. V. and A. P. Lukutins Factory, 1843-1863
The monogram "N" or "A" in the emblem refered to the reign
of Emperor Nicholas I (to 1855) or, respectively, Alexander II
(from 1855 to 1881)
(Version I)

P. V. and A. P. Lukutins Factory, 1843-1863
The monogram "N" or "A" in the emblem refered to the reign
of Emperor Nicholas I (to 1855) or, respectively, Alexander II
(from 1855 to 1881)
(Version II)

P. Lukutin Factory, 1863-1876
(Version I)

P. Lukutin Factory, 1863-1876
(Version II)

N. A. Lukutin Factory, 1888-1902
The monogram "A" or "N" in the emblem refered to the reign of Emperor Alexander III (from 1881 to 1894) or, respectively, Nicholas II (from 1894)
(Version I)

N. A. Lukutin Factory, 1888-1902
The monogram "A" or "N" in the emblem refered to the reign of Emperor Alexander III (from 1881 to 1894) or, respectively, Nicholas II (from 1894)
(Version II)

N. A. Lukutin Factory, 1896-1902

L. G. Lukutina Factory, Lukutin's heirs, 1902-1904

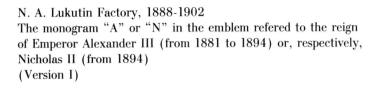

O. F. Vishnyakov and Sons Workshop, 1865-1870s

O. F. Vishnyakov and Sons Workshop, the 1870s
(Version I)

O. F. Vishnyakov and Sons Workshop, the 1870s
(Version II)

O. F. Vishnyakov and Sons Workshop, the 1870s
(Version III)

O. F. Vishnyakov and Sons Workshop, the early 1880s

V. O. Vishnyakov Workshop, 1877-the early 1880s

V. O. Vishnyakov Workshop, the 1880s

V. O. Vishnyakov Workshop, the late 1880s-the 1890s

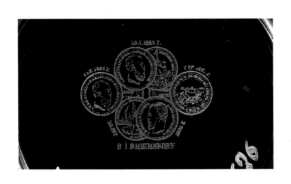

V. O. Vishnyakov Workshop, the 1890s

I. P. Vishnyakov Workshop, the mid-1880s

Fedoskino Artel of Former Lukutin Factory Masters,
after 1910 to the mid-1920s
(Version I)

Fedoskino Artel of Former Lukutin Factory Masters,
after 1910 to the mid-1920s
(Version II)

Fedoskino Painters' Artel, the 1950s

Fedoskino. Fedoskino Factory of Miniature Painting, from 1980s

Fedoskino Factory of Miniature Painting, the 1990s

Russkaya Kollektsia Association, from 1991

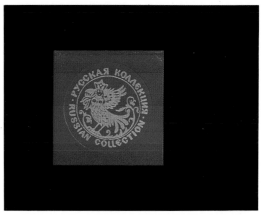

1. *Restaurant Scene* snuffbox
   P. I. Korobov Factory, early 19th century
   Papier-mache, oil, lacquer, painting, smoking
   Diam. 10.3; h. 1.8[1] SRM

2. Snuffbox with a portrait of the Grand Duke
   Constantin Pavlovich
   P. I. Korobov Factory, early 19th century
   Papier-mache, paper, engraving, lacquer
   Diam. 7; h. 2 SRM

3. *Poor Liza* snuffbox
   P. I. Korobov Factory, early 19th century
   Papier-mache, paper, engraving, lacquer
   Diam. 9.5; h. 2.2 SRM

4. *Cleopatra* snuffbox
   J. H. Stobwasser Factory, Germany, early 19th century
   Papier-mache, oil, lacquer, painting
   Diam. 8.5; h. 1.6 SRM

5. *Modest Young Girl* snuffbox
   P. I. Korobov Factory, early 19th century
   Papier-mache, oil, lacquer, painting
   Diam. 9.4; h. 2.2 SRM

6. *Angelica* snuffbox
   P. V. Lukutin Factory, the 1820s
   Papier-mache, oil, lacquer, painting
   Diam. 9.7; h. 2 SHM

7. *Lady in Turban* snuffbox
   P. V. Lukutin Factory, the 1830s
   Papier-mache, oil, lacquer, painting
   Diam. 9.5; h. 1.5 SHM

8. Alexander Osipovich Orlovsky (1777-1832)
   Messenger lithograph, 1821
   47x60 SRM

9. *Messenger* cigar-case
   P. V. Lukutin Factory, 1825-1828
   Papier-mache, gold leaf, oil, lacquer, painting
   8x13x2.5 PSMP

10. *Summer Troika* cigar-case
    P. V. and A. P. Lukutins Factory, the 1840s
    Papier-mache, oil, lacquer, painting
    5x8x1.5

11. *Horsemen* tray
    After A. O. Orlovsky
    P. V. Lukutin Factory, the 1830s
    Papier-mache, gold leaf, oil, lacquer, painting
    58.5x82x3.5 SRM

12. Set of travelling cups
    P. V. Lukutin Factory, the 1820s
    Papier-mache, painting in gold, oil, lacquer
    Diam. 8.5; h. 8 SHM

13. Cigar-case
    P. V. Lukutin Factory, the 1830s
    Papier-mache, foil, lacquer, guilloching
    13.7x6.5x4 SHM

14-18. *Good News* snuffbox
    P. V. Lukutin Factory, the 1830s
    Papier-mache, mother-of-pearl, oil, lacquer, painting
    5.5x8.5x4.5 SH

---

[1] All dimensions are given in centimetres.

19. *Under an Umbrella* cigar-case
P. V. Lukutin Factory, the 1820s
Papier-mache, oil, lacquer, painting
13.3x9.6x2.6   SHM

20. *Lake in the Mountains* snuffbox
P. V. Lukutin Factory, the 1820s
Papier-mache, oil, lacquer, painting
6.3x9.3x2   PSMP

21. *Count D. N. Sheremetev's Village of Ostankino* snuffbox
P. V. Lukutin Factory, the 1830s
Papier-mache, mother-of-pearl, oil, lacquer, painting
6.6x10x3.4   SRM

22. *Catherine* snuffbox
A. P. Lukutin Factory, the 1860s
Papier-mache, silver foil, oil, lacquer, painting
8.2x5x2.5   SHM

23. Snuffbox with a woman's portrait
O. F. Vishnyakov Workshop, the 1840s
Papier-mache, oil, lacquer, painting
8x5.3x1.8   RMDAFA

24. *Landscape with Fishermen* snuffbox
O. F. Vishnyakov Workshop, the 1840s
Papier-mache, oil, lacquer, painting
5.5x8.5x2.5   SRM

25. *A Lady with a Cavalier* snuffbox
O. F. Vishnyakov Workshop, the 1840s
Papier-mache, oil, lacquer, painting
Diam. 8.2; h. 2.2   SHM

26. *Boys Feeding Puppies* cigar-case with matchbox
O. F. Vishnyakov Workshop, the 1860s

Papier-mache, oil, lacquer, painting
13x7.3x1.7   PSMP

27. *Emperor Nicholas I, Grand Duke Mikhail Pavlovich, Tsesarevich Alexander Nikolayevich, Prince P. M. Volkonsky and Count A. K. Benkendorf* cigar-case
G. Morcelli after an original by F. Kruger
P. V. Lukutin Factory, the 1830s
Papier-mache, paper, watercolour, gouache, lacquer
15x9x2.5   SRM

28. *Emperor Nicholas I Hunting* snuffbox
P. V. Lukutin Factory, the 1830s
Papier-mache, mother-of-pearl, oil, lacquer, painting
9x5.7x1.7   SRM

29. *Emperor Nicholas I and Empress Alexandra Fedorovna with Their Son* snuffbox
P. V. Lukutin Factory, the 1830s
Papier-mache, oil, lacquer, painting
6.8x10.2x2.7   SRM

30. Engraving with a Portrait of Tsar Alexei Mikhailovich, 1817
After an original by A. Benner
18x15   SRM

31. Snuffbox with a Portrait of Tsar Alexei Mikhailovich
P. V. and A. P. Lukutins Factory, the 1850s
Papier-mache, oil, lacquer, painting
7.7x5x3.3   SRM

32. Engraving with a Portrait of Alexander I, 1817
After an original by A. Benner
18x14.5   SRM

33. Snuffbox with a Portrait of Alexander I
P. V. and A. P. Lukutins Factory, the 1850s
Papier-mache, oil, lacquer, painting
7.7x5.3x4 SRM

34. Engraving with a Portrait of Tsarevna Sofia, 1817
After an original by A. Benner
18x15 SRM

35. Snuffbox with a Portrait of Tsarevna Sofia
P. V. and A. P. Lukutins Factory, the 1850s
Papier-mache, gold leaf, oil, lacquer, painting
9.5x5x3.3 PSMP

36. Snuffbox with a Portrait of Count M. S. Vorontsov
P. V. and A. P. Lukutins Factory, the 1850s
Papier-mache, oil, lacquer, painting
9.7x4.5x3 RLI

37. *Homer with the Muse* snuffbox
P. V. and A. P. Lukutins Factory, the 1850s
Papier-mache, oil, lacquer, painting, *skan'*
4.7x9x3.5 SRM

38. *Young Girl in Yellow* snuffbox
P. V. and A. P. Lukutins Factory, the 1850s
Papier-mache, oil, lacquer, painting
7.7x6x3.5 SRM

39. *Artist's Family* snuffbox
P. V. and A. P. Lukutins Factory, the 1840s
Papier-mache, oil, lacquer, painting
8.5x5.5x2.7 SHM

40. *Berta and Serafina* snuffbox
P. V. and A. P. Lukutins Factory, the 1840s
Papier-mache, oil, lacquer, painting
8.8x6.5x3 PSMP

41. *Young Girl with a Kitten* snuffbox
P. V. and A. P. Lukutins Factory, the 1840s
Papier-mache, oil, lacquer, painting in gold
5x8.5x3 SHM

42. Snuffbox
P. V. and A. P. Lukutins Factory, the 1840s
Papier-mache, oil, lacquer, painting in gold and silver
5.8x8.5x4 SHM

43. Snuffbox with Chinoiserie
P. V. and A. P. Lukutins Factory, the 1840s
Papier-mache, gold leaf, oil, lacquer, relief, painting
5.7x8.5x2.7 SH

44. *Girls with Camomiles* snuffbox
P. V. and A. P. Lukutins Factory, the 1850s
Papier-mache, metal powder, gold, oil, lacquer, painting
5.7x8.2x3.5 SRM

45. *Listening to a Song* box
P. V. and A. P. Lukutins Factory, the 1850s
Papier-mache, metal powder, gold leaf, oil, lacquer,
painting
14x20x8 SHM

46. *Wreath* snuffbox
P. V. and A. P. Lukutins Factory, the 1850s
Papier-mache, metal powder, gold, oil, lacquer, painting
7.5x3.5x5 SHM

47. *Bird in a Cage* snuffbox
A. P. Lukutin Factory, the 1860s
Papier-mache, oil, lacquer, painting
Diam. 9.75; h. 1.75 SHM

48. *Young Girl with a Book* cigar-case
P. V. and A. P. Lukutins Factory, the 1850s
Papier-mache, metal powder, gold, oil, lacquer, painting
17x8x2.5 RMDAFA

49. *Would You Like a Drink?* cigarette-case
P. V. and A. P. Lukutins Factory, the 1850s
Papier-mache, oil, lacquer, relief, painting
7x12.5x2.2 SHM

50. *Dance* album
Workshop of the Vishnyakovs's Circle, the 1880s
Papier-mache, metal powder, oil, lacquer, painting
21x30x5 RMDAFA

51. *Fandango* snuffbox
P. V. and A. P. Lukutins Factory, the 1830s
Papier-mache, mother-of-pearl, oil, lacquer, painting
6x8.8x3.3 SRM

52. *Angelica* snuffbox
P. V. Lukutin Factory, the 1830s
Papier-mache, oil, lacquer, painting
8.8x6x4 SRM

53. Snuffbox for two types of tobacco
P. V. and A. P. Lukutins Factory, the 1850s
Papier-mache, oil, lacquer, painting
4x7.5x5.5 SHM

54. *Ornamental* cigar-case
P. V. Lukutin Factory, the 1830s
Papier-mache, foil, lacquer, guilloching
13x7.7x2.3 SH

55. Snuffbox with a Portrait of Ivan Krylov
After an engraving of K. A. Bryullov's original
P. V. and A. P. Lukutins Factory, the 1850s
Papier-mache, oil, lacquer, painting, *skan'*
7.7x5.3x3.5 SRM

56. Purse
Workshop of the Vishnyakovs's Circle, the 1870s
Papier-mache, oil, lacquer, painting
5x7.5x2 SRM

57. Inlaid snuffbox
P. V. and A. P. Lukutins Factory, the 1840s
Papier-mache, mother-of-pearl, lacquer
4.7x9.7x4 SRM

58. *Girls with a Dog* snuffbox
P. V. and A. P. Lukutins Factory, the 1840s
Papier-mache, oil, lacquer, painting
2.5x3.5x1.5 SRM

59. Cigar-case with Sheremetevs' Coat of Arms
P. V. Lukutin Factory, the 1830s
Papier-mache, mother-of-pearl, gold leaf, oil, lacquer, painting
13.6x9x2.7 SH

60. *Grandmother's Tales* snuffbox
A. P. Lukutin Factory, the 1850s
Papier-mache, gold leaf, oil, lacquer, painting, relief
4.8x9.7x3.5 SRM

61. Cigar-case with guilloching
P. V. Lukutin Factory, the 1830s
Papier-mache, foil, lacquer, guilloching
13.7x6.5x4 SRM

62. *At a Water Spring* snuffbox
P. V. and A. P. Lukutins Factory, the 1840s
Papier-mache, mother-of-pearl, oil, lacquer, painting
4.8x9.3x4 SRM

63. Vassily Fedorovich Timm (1820-1895)
Emperor Alexander Nikolayevich and Empress Maria Alexandrovna, lithograph, 1858
30x41 SRM

64. *Emperor Alexander II and the Empress in a Sledge* box
A. P. Lukutin Factory, the 1860s
Papier-mache, oil, lacquer, painting
8x13x3.5 SHM

65. *Winter Troika* box
V. O. Vishnyakov Workshop, the 1880s
Papier-mache, metal powder, oil, lacquer, painting
9.7x15x11 SRM

66. *Winter Troika* box
I. P. Vishnyakov Workshop, the 1890s
Papier-mache, metal powder, oil, lacquer, painting
8.5x13.5x7.6 SRM

67. *Winter Troika* pencil-holder
V. O. Vishnyakov Workshop, the 1880s
Papier-mache, metal powder, oil, lacquer, painting
Diam. 8; h. 7.5 PSMP

68. *Winter Troika* pencil-holder
V. O. Vishnyakov Workshop, the 1880s
Papier-mache, metal powder, oil, lacquer, painting
Diam. 7.5; h. 9.5 SRM

69. *Winter Troika* snuffbox
Workshop of the Vishnyakovs' Circle, the 1880s
Papier-mache, metal powder, oil, lacquer, painting
3x3.2x2 SRM

70. *A Ukrainian Woman*, lithograph, 1861
After a drawing by I. I. Sokolov
40x30.5 SRM

71. *A Ukrainian Woman with a Yoke* matchbox
A. P. Lukutin Factory, the 1860s
Papier-mache, oil, lacquer, painting
6.2x3.8x2 SRM

72. *A Ukrainian Woman with a Yoke* box
V. O. Vishnyakov Workshop, the 1880s
Papier-mache, metal powder, oil, lacquer, painting
Diam. 5.5; h. 3 SRM

73. *A Ukrainian Woman* blotting-case
O. F. Vishnyakov Workshop, the 1870s
Papier-mache, metal powder, gold leaf, oil, lacquer, painting
30x23x2 SRM

74. Rudolf Kazimirovich Zhukovsky (1814-1886)
Returning from a Fair, lithograph, 1841
22x17.5 SRM

75. *Returning from a Fair* box
A. P. Lukutin Factory, the 1860s
Papier-mache, metal powder, oil, lacquer, painting
Diam. 9.7; h. 8.5 SHM

76. *Merry-Making* album
A. P. Lukutin Factory, the 1870s
Papier-mache, metal powder, oil, lacquer, painting
16.5x14.5x6 SRM

77. *Merry-Making* snuffbox
O. F. Vishnyakov Workshop, the 1860s
Papier-mache, metal powder, oil, lacquer, painting
4.2x7.6x3 SRM

78. Easter Egg
N. A. Lukutin Factory, the 1890s
Papier-mache, metal powder, gold leaf, oil, lacquer, painting
Diam. 10.6; h. 16 SRM

79. *Trinity* icon
    N. A. Lukutin Factory, the 1900s
    Papier-mache, gold leaf, oil, lacquer, painting
    18x12x0.3   SRM

80. Easter Egg
    A. P. Lukutin Factory, 1866
    Papier-mache, metal powder, gold leaf, oil, lacquer,
    painting
    Diam. 6.5; h. 10   SRM

81. Easter Egg
    A. P. Lukutin Factory, 1867
    Papier-mache, metal powder, gold leaf, oil, lacquer,
    painting
    Diam. 6.5; h. 9.8   SRM

82. *Tea-drinking* matchbox
    V. O. Vishnyakov Workshop, the 1880s
    Papier-mache, metal powder, oil, lacquer, painting
    Diam. 11; h. 12   SRM

83. *Tea-drinking* keg
    A. P. Lukutin Factory, the 1860s
    Papier-mache, metal powder, oil, lacquer, painting
    Diam. 9.5; h. 8.5   SRM

84. *Tea-drinking* snuffbox
    A. P. Lukutin Factory, the 1860s
    Papier-mache, metal powder, oil, lacquer, painting
    7.7x3.5x2.5   SRM

85. *Tryst by a Hut* purse
    After a drawing by K. A. Trutovsky
    A. P. Lukutin Factory, the 1880s
    Papier-mache, metal powder, oil, lacquer, painting
    8.6x6.7x2   SRM

86. *Demian's Fish Soup* cigarette-case
    V. O. Vishnyakov Workshop, the 1870s
    Papier-mache, metal powder, oil, lacquer, painting
    10.2x15x16   SRM

87. Paul-Marie Roussel (1804-1877)
    A Happy Family, lithograph, 1840
    22x17.6   SRM

88. *A Happy Family* keg
    A. P. Lukutin Factory, the 1860s
    Papier-mache, silver and gold foil, oil, lacquer, painting
    Diam. 10.2; h. 9.5   SRM

89. *Drum* box
    O. F. Vishnyakov Workshop, the 1880s
    Papier-mache, gold leaf, oil, lacquer, painting
    Diam. 13; h. 12.5   SRM

90. *Malachite* tea-caddy
    V. O. Vishnyakov Workshop, the 1890s
    Papier-mache, oil, lacquer, painting
    12.5x12.5x13.2   SRM

91. *Dance* keg
    Unknown Workshop of the Vishnyakovs' Circle, the 1890s
    Papier-mache, metal powder, oil, lacquer, painting
    Diam. 11.5; h. 10.5   SRM

92. *Round Dance* plate
    O. F. Vishnyakov Workshop, the 1880s
    Papier-mache, metal powder, oil, lacquer, painting
    Diam. 21.5; h. 2   PSMP

93. *Abduction* keg
    P. O. Vishnyakov Workshop, the 1880s
    Papier-mache, metal powder, oil, lacquer, painting
    Diam. 10.5; h. 12   RMDAFA

94. *Winter Troika* casket
O. F. Vishnyakov Workshop, the 1880s
Papier-mache, metal powder, oil, lacquer, painting
14.5x19x10.3   RMDAFA

95. *Hunter* keg
V. O. Vishnyakov Workshop, the 1880s
Papier-mache, oil, lacquer, painting
Diam. 5.5; h. 4.5   SRM

96. *Snow-storm* powder-box
A. P. and N. A. Lukutins Factory, the 1880s
Papier-mache, metal powder, oil, lacquer, painting
Diam. 8.5; h. 3   PSMP

97. *Riverside House* snuffbox
V. O. Vishnyakov Workshop, the 1880s
Papier-mache, oil, lacquer, painting
6x8.6x2.7   SRM

98. *Landscape with a Bridge* snuffbox
V. O. Vishnyakov Workshop, the 1880s
Papier-mache, oil, lacquer, painting
6x8.5x2.5   SRM

99. Card-case
O. F. Vishnyakov Workshop, the 1880s
Papier-mache, oil, lacquer, painting
10x13x3   SRM

100. *Riverside Houses* table-matchbox
V. O. Vishnyakov Workshop, the 1880s
Papier-mache, oil, lacquer, painting
8.5x8.5x6.2   SRM

101. *Winter Sledges* box
Master Vishnyakov, the 1890s
Papier-mache, metal powder, oil, lacquer, painting
Diam. 17.5; h. 8.5   SRM

102. Box in imitation of tortoise-shell
V. O. Vishnyakov Workshop, the 1870s
Papier-mache, oil, lacquer, painting
11x14.5x4   SRM

103. *Winter Troika* casket
O. F. Vishnyakov Workshop, the 1880s
Papier-mache, metal powder, oil, lacquer, painting
12.6x14x7.5   SRM

104. *Mandore-player and a Spinner* album
V. O. Vishnyakov Workshop, the 1890s
Papier-mache, metal powder, oil, lacquer, painting
27x22.5x7   SRM

105. Stamp-box
O. F. Vishnyakov Workshop, the 1880s
Papier-mache, oil, lacquer, painting
5.3x11.3x3   SRM

106. Napkin ring
Workshop of the Vishnyakovs' Circle, the 1890s
Papier-mache, oil, lacquer, painting
3.5x6x4   SRM

107. Album plate
Workshop of the Vishnyakovs' Circle, the 1880s
Papier-mache, oil, lacquer, painting
24x18.5x0.3   SRM

108. Paper-weight
N. A. Lukutin Factory, the 1890s
Papier-mache, metal powder, oil, lacquer, painting
8x13x3   SRM

109. Napkin ring
Workshop of the Vishnyakovs' Circle, the 1890s
Papier-mache, oil, lacquer, painting
Diam. 5.5; h. 4   SRM

110. Napkin ring
V. O. Vishnyakov Workshop, the 1880s
Papier-mache, oil, lacquer, painting
Diam. 5.5; h. 4   SRM

111. Card-table brush
Workshop of the Vishnyakovs' Circle, the 1890s
Papier-mache, oil, lacquer, painting
Diam. 5.7; h. 3   SRM

112. *Dance* cigar-case
O. F. Vishnyakov Workshop, the 1860s
Papier-mache, metal powder, oil, lacquer, painting
9.5x5x2.3   SRM

113. *Summer Troika* box
O. F. Vishnyakov Workshop, the 1870s
Papier-mache, metal powder, oil, lacquer, painting
11.5x18x10.5   SRM

114. Stepan Gavrilovich Platonov (village of Nikulskoye)
Winter Sledges album plate, the 1880s
Papier-mache, metal powder, gold leaf, oil, lacquer, painting
30.7x24.5x0.3   SRM

115. *Mummers with a Bear* casket
V. O. Vishnyakov Workshop, the 1890s
Papier-mache, metal powder, oil, lacquer, painting
10.3x15x6   SRM

116. *Winter Night* biscuit dish
V. O. Vishnyakov Workshop, the 1890s
Iron, gold leaf, oil, lacquer, painting
Diam. 26.6; h. 4.3   SRM

117. *Winter Troika* cigar-case
Burbyshevs' Workshop, after 1910
Silver, chrysoprase, oil, lacquer, painting
8.5x11.3x1.2   SRM

118. *Summer Holiday in Ukraine* box
Novoseltsevo Village Workshop, the 1880s
Papier-mache, oil, lacquer, painting
11.6x22.3x10.6

119. *After Mowing* biscuit dish
N. A. Lukutin Factory, the 1890s
Papier-mache, metal powder, oil, lacquer, painting
Diam. 24; h. 8   SRM

120. *Damsel by a Hedge* box
After an original by K. E. Makovsky
N. A. Lukutin Factory, the 1890s
Papier-mache, metal powder, gold leaf, oil, lacquer, painting
15x24x8   SRM

121. *Young Girls Telling Fortune by Wreaths* box
N. A. Lukutin Factory, the 1890s
Papier-mache, oil, lacquer, painting
18.8x37.4x8   SRM

122. *Attacking Wolves* box
Fedoskino Artel, the 1930s
Papier-mache, oil, lacquer, painting
10.2x15x10.2   SRM

123. Box with a silhouette picture
Fedoskino Artel of Former Lukutin Factory Masters, after 1910
Papier-mache, bronze powder, oil, lacquer, painting
9x14x4.3   SRM

124. Nikolai Semenovich Semenov (1883-1950)
Shepherd box, the 1930s
Papier-mache, oil, lacquer, painting
Diam. 17; h. 6   FFF

125. Mikhail Kuzmich Papenov (1889-1952)
To a Fair box, 1946
Papier-mache, oil, lacquer, painting
12.5x22x8.5   FFF

126. Ivan Ivanovich Bannov (1913-1943)
Station-master plate, 1937
Papier-mache, oil, lacquer, painting
15x20x0.7   RPM

127. Konstantin Ivanovich Zorin (1916-1941)
Pushkin among the Decembrists box, 1937
After an original by D. N. Kardovsky
Papier-mache, oil, lacquer, painting
11x16x5   RPM

128. Mikhail Stepanovich Chizhov (1923-1986)
Lay of Igor's Host casket
Papier-mache, metal powder, gold leaf, oil, lacquer, painting
14.7x22x10.5   RLI

129. Valentin Nikolayevich Samsonov (b. 1927)
Bayan Poet box, 1950
Papier-mache, oil, lacquer, painting
12x12x9.5   RLI

130. Mikhail Stepanovich Chizhov (1923-1986)
Harvest-woman box, 1950
Papier-mache, oil, lacquer, painting
15.5x11.2x5   SRM

131. Mikhail Grigorievich Pashinin (b. 1921)
Russian Dance case, 1957
Papier-mache, gold leaf, oil, lacquer, painting
13.7x8.7x4.5   FFF

132. Yuri Vasilievich Gusev (b. 1933)
Evenings Outside Moscow casket, 1958
Papier-mache, mother-of-pearl, oil, lacquer, painting
22.5x29x9.5   FFF

133. Mikhail Stepanovich Chizhov (1923-1986)
Liberation of Volokolamsk box, 1966
Papier-mache, oil, lacquer, painting
10.3x13.3x3.3   SRM

134. Mikhail Stepanovich Chizhov (1923-1986)
Fedoskino. Winter casket, 1968
Papier-mache, oil, lacquer, painting
11.7x14.5x4.7   SRM

135. Ivan Ivanovich Strakhov (1918-1979)
Landscape with a Bridge casket, 1957
Papier-mache, gold leaf, oil, lacquer, painting
10x16x6   SRM

136. Ivan Ivanovich Strakhov (1918-1979)
Landscape with a Cabin box, 1969
Papier-mache, gold leaf, oil, lacquer, painting
7.5x10.5x2.5   FFF

137. Sergei Petrovich Rogatov (b. 1920)
After Rain box, 1989
Papier-mache, aluminum powder, oil, lacquer, painting
11x6.5x3.5

138. Lydia Alexandrovna Stroganova (b. 1938)
After Reaping box, 1989
Papier-mache, oil, lacquer, painting
4.5x10.5x2   SRM

139. Sergei Sergeyevich Rogatov (b. 1955)
Autumn box, 1988
Papier-mache, gold leaf, oil, lacquer, painting
16x3.2x4.5   SRM

140. Sergei Petrovich Rogatov (b. 1920)
Landscape. Fedoskino casket, 1990
Papier-mache, oil, lacquer, painting
11.5x22.5x6.5

141. Viktor Dmitrievich Lipitsky (1921-1994)
Night in the Village casket, 1979
Papier-mache, gold leaf, oil, lacquer, painting
10x12x5   FFF

142. Mikhail Grigorievich Pashinin (b. 1921)
Pushkin Visiting Gogol box, 1981
Papier-mache, aluminum powder, oil, lacquer, painting
8x11x3

143. Viktor Ivanovich Tretyakov (b. 1955)
Great Russians casket, 1994
After an original by H.-F. C. Pauli
Papier-mache, oil, lacquer, painting
Diam. 7.5; h. 4.5

144. Mikhail Grigorievich Pashinin (b. 1921)
Pushkin on the Neva box, 1956
Papier-mache, oil, lacquer, painting
8.3x5.5x5   RPM

145. Mikhail Iosifovich Kornienko (b. 1926)
Church of the Intercession on the Nerl box, 1987
Papier-mache, mother-of-pearl, gold leaf, oil, lacquer, painting
Diam. 8; h. 6

146. Nadezhda Viktorovna Strelkina (Burbysheva) (b. 1960)
Scarlet Flower box, 1990
Papier-mache, aluminum powder, gold leaf, oil, lacquer, painting
6.3x8x3.5   FFF

147. Viktor Ivanovich Tretyakov (b. 1955)
On a Walk case, 1994
Papier-mache, oil, lacquer, painting
10.7x7.5x4.3   FFF

148. Gennady Venediktovich Skripunov (b. 1923)
Kirill-Belozersky Monastery casket, 1991
Papier-mache, aluminum powder, gold leaf, oil, lacquer, painting
7.8x22.5x5

149. Gennady Venediktovich Skripunov (b. 1923)
Russian Winter box, 1994
Papier-mache, oil, lacquer, painting
5x13.6x4

150. Gennady Venediktovich Skripunov (b. 1923)
Early Snow box, 1993
Papier-mache, aluminum powder, oil, lacquer, painting
4.6x6.2x4.3

151. Yevgeni Sergeyevich Shishkin (b. 1940)
Winter Night. Fedoskino casket, 1993
Papier-mache, mother-of-pearl, aluminum powder, oil, lacquer, painting
13x19x6   FFF

152. Sergei Vasilievich Monashov (b. 1923)
Festive box, 1992
Papier-mache, foil, lacquer, *skan'*
5.3x4x6

153. Sergei Vasilievich Monashov (b. 1923)
Peacock Feather keg, 1989
Papier-mache, foil, lacquer, *skan'*
Diam. 5.8; h. 4.5

154. Sergei Vasilievich Monashov (b. 1923)
Oval case, 1993
Papier-mache, foil, lacquer, *skan'*
8x4.5x3.5

155. Yuri Vasilievich Gusev (b. 1933)
Blue Wave box, 1983
Papier-mache, foil, lacquer, *skan'*
7.8x6x4   SRM

156. Vladimir Olegovich Kalinin (b. 1967)
Still Life box, 1992
Papier-mache, foil, oil, lacquer, painting, *skan'*
7x7x4   FFF

157. Nikolai Georgievich Marchukov (b. 1936)
Pskov Kremlin box, 1994
Papier-mache, aluminum powder, gold leaf, oil, lacquer, painting
6x9x4.5

158. Svetlana Petrovna Marchukova (b. 1932)
Alexander Gavrilovich Golikov (b. 1927) (jeweller)
Winter Troika brooch, 1993
Papier-mache, gold leaf, oil, lacquer, painting, filigree
Diam. 5.5; h. 0.5

159. Svetlana Petrovna Marchukova (b. 1932)
Alexander Gavrilovich Golikov (b. 1927) (jeweller)
Summer Troika brooch, 1993
Papier-mache, gold leaf, oil, lacquer, painting, filigree
4x7x0.5

160. Lyubov Nikolayevna Krasnoslobodtseva (b. 1964)
Little Khavroshechka box, 1994
Papier-mache, gold leaf, oil, lacquer, painting
3.7x5x3

161. Nikolai Mikhailovich Soloninkin (b. 1945)
Casket with a Portrait of Mikhail Lomonosov, 1991
Papier-mache, mother-of-pearl, gold, oil, lacquer, *skan'*
25.8x18.8x9.8   FFF

162. Nikolai Mikhailovich Soloninkin (b. 1945)
Boris Nikolayevich Korneyev (b. 1938) (jeweller)
Medallion with a Portrait of Tsar Mikhail Fedorovich, 1995
Papier-mache, silver, oil, lacquer, painting, filigree
9.5x8.5x0.8

163. Nikolai Mikhailovich Soloninkin (b. 1945)
Boris Nikolayevich Korneyev (b. 1938) (jeweller)
Medallion with a Portrait of Empress Catherine II, 1995
Papier-mache, oil, lacquer, painting, filigree
9.5x8.5x0.8

164. Nikolai Mikhailovich Soloninkin (b. 1945)
Boris Nikolayevich Korneyev (b. 1938) (jeweller)
Medallion with a Portrait of Emperor Nicholas I, 1995
Papier-mache, oil, lacquer, painting, filigree
9.5x8.5x0.8

165. Nikolai Mikhailovich Soloninkin (b. 1945)
Boris Nikolayevich Korneyev (b. 1938) (jeweller)
Medallion with a Portrait of Emperor Alexander III, 1995
Papier-mache, oil, lacquer, painting, filigree
9.5x8.5x0.8

166. Petr Nikolayevich Puchkov (b. 1932)
Evening Bells (Trinity-Sergius Lavra) casket, 1991
Papier-mache, mother-of-pearl, gold leaf, oil, lacquer,
painting
22x28.5x9   FFF

167. Viktor Danilovich Antonov (b. 1936)
Fedoskino Landscapes casket, 1994
Papier-mache, oil, lacquer, painting
17x16x11

168. Vladimir Viktorovich Rogatov (b. 1961)
The Great Reformer set of caskets, 1994
Papier-mache, oil, lacquer, painting, smoking
21.5x13.5x6.5; 8.5x5.2x2

169. Dmitri Viktorovich Rogatov (b. 1956)
Tryst in a Summer House case, 1995
Papier-mache, mother-of-pearl, gold leaf, aluminum
powder, oil, lacquer, painting
10.5x5.5x3

170. Nadezhda Viktorovna Strelkina (Burbysheva) (b. 1960)
Day and Night box, 1994
Papier-mache, mother-of-pearl, gold leaf, oil, lacquer,
painting
6x4x4

171. Nadezhda Viktorovna Strelkina (Burbysheva) (b. 1960)
Pretty Lasses box, 1994
Papier-mache, mother-of-pearl, gold leaf, oil, lacquer,
painting
7x5x3.5

172. Vladimir Viktorovich Rogatov (b. 1961)
In an Old Park box, 1995
Papier-mache, mother-of-pearl, gold leaf, oil, lacquer,
painting
Diam. 5.2; h. 7.5

173. Alexei Viktorovich Korchagin (b. 1960)
Dedicated to Gogol triptych (boxes *Great-coat, Dead
Souls* and *The Nose*), 1995
Papier-mache, oil, lacquer, painting
7x13x8.5; 9x6.5x6

174. Andrei Andreyevich Moshchevitin (b. 1957)
Grandfather Yegor casket, 1991
Papier-mache, gold leaf, oil, lacquer, painting
8.5x10x4.2

175. Andrei Andreyevich Moshchevitin (b. 1957)
August casket, 1983
Papier-mache, foil, oil, lacquer, painting, *skan'*
8.5x11.5x5

176. Andrei Andreyevich Moshchevitin (b. 1957)
Backwater casket, 1992
Papier-mache, oil, lacquer, painting
4.5x5.7x3.4

177. Andrei Andreyevich Moshchevitin (b. 1957)
Evening casket, 1992
Papier-mache, oil, lacquer, painting
3.8x9.8x2.3

178. Yevgenia Albertovna Moshchevitina (b. 1960)
Flowers casket, 1992
Papier-mache, gold leaf, oil, lacquer, painting
Diam. 4.5; h. 6.3

179. Alexander Alexandrovich Fedorov (b. 1957)
Autumn Coming casket, 1993
Papier-mache, gold leaf, mother-of-pearl, oil, lacquer,
painting
4.7x8.7x2.8

180. Alexander Alexandrovich Fedorov (b. 1957)
Signs of Spring casket, 1992
Papier-mache, mother-of-pearl, oil, lacquer, painting
4.5x5.5x2.2

181. Yuri Vasilievich Karapayev (b. 1936)
Darling casket, 1994
Papier-mache, aluminum powder, gold leaf, oil, lacquer,
painting
14.5x12x5

182. Alla Anatolievna Kozlova (b. 1958)
Case, 1992
Papier-mache, gold leaf, mother-of-pearl, oil, lacquer,
painting
7x6x3

183. Lyubov Sergeyevna Rogatova (b. 1960)
By the Well case, 1994
Papier-mache, aluminum powder, gold leaf, oil, lacquer,
painting
9.7x7x3.5

184. Yuri Vasilievich Karapayev (b. 1936)
Tryst box, 1980
Papier-mache, mother-of-pearl, aluminum powder, oil,
lacquer, painting
10.3x5x3   FFF

185. Sergei Ivanovich Kozlov (b. 1955)
Alexander Pushkin and Natalia Goncharova casket, 1993
Papier-mache, mother-of-pearl, gold leaf, oil, lacquer,
painting
Diam. 8; h. 16

186. Sergei Ivanovich Kozlov (b. 1955)
Winter at Sergiev Posad casket, 1994

Papier-mache, gold leaf, oil, lacquer, painting
13x6x3.5

187. Yuri Vasilievich Karapayev (b. 1936)
April casket, 1984
Papier-mache, mother-of-pearl, oil, lacquer, painting
10.5x13.5x6   SRM

188. Gennady Ivanovich Larishev (b. 1929)
Halloo, Halloo, Annushka casket, 1991
Papier-mache, mother-of-pearl, gold leaf, oil, lacquer,
painting
14x21x6.5   FFF

189. Oleg Ivanovich Shapkin (b. 1955)
Dream box, 1995
Papier-mache, oil, lacquer, painting
11x11x13.5

190. Oleg Ivanovich Shapkin (b. 1955)
Pushkin and Gypsies case, 1994
Papier-mache, mother-of-pearl, oil, lacquer, painting
10x15x4.6

191. Sergei Sergeyevich Rogatov (b. 1955)
St. Basil's Cathedral casket, 1994
Papier-mache, gold, mother-of-pearl, oil, lacquer, painting
19x15x6

192. Nikolai Alexandrovich Zotov (b. 1960)
Winter tea-caddy, 1988
Papier-mache, mother-of-pearl, oil, lacquer, painting
8x7.5x6   FFF

193. Viktoria Valerievna Sinelnikova (Kuzmenko) (b. 1968)
At the Skating-Rink casket, 1994
Papier-mache, oil, lacquer, painting
8.5x13.5x6

194. Mikhail Alexandrovich Tugarinov (b. 1957)
Marfino casket, 1991
Papier-mache, bronze powder, oil, lacquer, painting
5.5x10.5x3.7 RKF

195. Valery Sergeyevich Kovalev (b. 1963)
Winter Troika casket, 1993
Papier-mache, bronze powder, oil, lacquer, painting
4.5x10x4 RKF

196. Sergei Sergeyevich Chistov (b. 1946)
Yemelya casket, 1993
Papier-mache, aluminum powder, mother-of-pearl, oil,
lacquer, painting
9.5x9.5x4

197. Valery Sergeyevich Kovalev (b. 1963)
Night box, 1994
Papier-mache, aluminum powder, oil, lacquer, painting
5x4x2

198. Igor Alexandrovich Isayev (b. 1956)
Tea-drinking case, 1992
Papier-mache, gold leaf, oil, lacquer, painting, *skan'*
3.5x7x3.5

199. Nikolai Alexandrovich Zotov (b. 1960)
Bird Cherry box, 1993
Papier-mache, gold leaf, oil, lacquer, painting
7x5x3.3 FFF

200. Vladimir Nikolayevich Domakhin (b. 1963)
Water-carrier casket, 1990
Papier-mache, aluminum powder, gold dissolved in gum
arabic, oil, lacquer, painting
5x12x4 RKF

201. Vladimir Nikolayevich Domakhin (b. 1963)
Bad News casket, 1994
Papier-mache, aluminum powder, gold dissolved in gum
arabic, oil, lacquer, painting
7.5x12x4

202. Sergei Sergeyevich Rogatov (b. 1955)
Night in the Village box, 1994
Papier-mache, oil, lacquer, painting
4x9x9 RKF

203. Marina Serafimovna Rogatova (b. 1962)
At a Tea-House casket, 1993
Papier-mache, oil, lacquer, painting
5.3x6x3.8 RKF

204. Viktoria Valerievna Sinelnikova (Kuzmenko) (b. 1968)
A Couple box, 1994
Papier-mache, gold, oil, lacquer, painting
11x5.2x4

205. Yelena Yurievna Khomutinnikova (b. 1957)
Morning box, 1994
Papier-mache, oil, lacquer, painting
12.5x5x3

206. Valery Sergeyevich Kovalev (b. 1963)
Wedding casket, 1993
Papier-mache, oil, lacquer, painting, filigree
5x7x4

207. Igor Alexandrovich Isayev (b. 1956)
At a Fabric Shop box, 1993
Papier-mache, mother-of-pearl, oil, lacquer, *skan'*
5.3x4.3x2.8

208. Maria Sergeyevna Wagner (b. 1950)
Meeting a Guest box, 1990
Papier-mache, gold leaf, aluminum powder, oil, lacquer, painting
3.2x7x2.2   FFF

209. Nikolai Alexandrovich Zotov (b. 1960)
Tsarevna the Frog casket, 1989
Papier-mache, oil, lacquer, painting
3.5x5.5x3.3   FFF

210. Vladimir Nikolayevich Domakhin (b. 1963)
Peasant Wedding casket, 1990
Papier-mache, aluminum powder, oil, lacquer, painting
9.5x14x4   RKF

211. Viktoria Valerievna Sinelnikova (Kuzmenko) (b. 1968)
Marfino case, 1993
Papier-mache, oil, lacquer, painting
11.5x5.5x2.7

212. Sergei Ivanovich Kozlov (b. 1955)
Marfino casket, 1987
Papier-mache, oil, lacquer, painting
7x8x5.5   SRM

213. Valery Sergeyevich Kovalev (b. 1963)
Winter Troikas casket, 1992
Papier-mache, oil, lacquer, painting
7x17x4.5   RKF

214. Inna Valerievna Kombarova (b. 1960)
An Apprentice box, 1994
Papier-mache, gold leaf, oil, lacquer, painting
5.5x9.5x3.5

215 Viktor Danilovich Antonov (b. 1936)
Indian Summer casket, 1994

Papier-mache, gold leaf, oil, lacquer, painting
6x11x2.5

216. Dmitri Viktorovich Rogatov (b. 1956)
Russian Icarus casket, 1991
Papier-mache, gold leaf, oil, lacquer, painting
17.5x7.5x4   RKF

217. Mikhail Iosifovich Kornienko (b. 1926)
Fedoskino Landscape at Night box, 1994
Papier-mache, oil, lacquer, painting
5.5x8x3.5

218. Alexander Alexeyevich Tolstov (b. 1929)
Winter box, 1981
Papier-mache, mother-of-pearl, oil, lacquer, painting
4.5x6.5x2   SRM

219. Alexander Alexandrovich Fedorov (b. 1957)
An Old Bridge casket, 1988
Papier-mache, gold leaf, oil, lacquer, painting
11x8x2.5

220. Alexander Alexandrovich Fedorov (b. 1957)
In the Woods casket, 1987
Papier-mache, gold leaf, mother-of-pearl, oil, lacquer, painting, *skan'*
10x6.5x4.5

221. Yuri Vasilievich Gusev (b. 1933)
Casket, 1988
Papier-mache, gold, painting
Diam. 8; h. 3.5   FFF

222. Yuri Vasilievich Gusev (b. 1933)
Fireworks casket, 1984
Papier-mache, lacquer, *skan'*
Diam. 7.5; h. 3

223. Yuri Vasilievich Gusev (b. 1933)
Case, 1987
Papier-mache, lacquer, *skan'*
3x12x2.5

224. Andrei Andreyevich Moshchevitin (b. 1957)
Winter Forest decorative panel, 1993
Papier-mache, mahogany, aluminum powder,
gold leaf, oil, lacquer, painting
22.5x17.5x1.5

Page 5:
Winter Troika snuffbox
A. P. Lukutin Factory, the 1860s
Papier-mache, metal powder, oil, lacquer, painting
4.5x10x3.5   RLI

Dust-cover back:
Dmitri Viktorovich Rogatov (b. 1956)
Walking to the Well casket, 1980
Papier-mache, gold leaf, aluminum powder, oil, lacquer,
painting
10x6x4.5

List of Abbreviations

SRM

State Russian Museum, St. Petersburg

SH

State Hermitage, St. Petersburg

SHM

State History Museum, Moscow

FFF

Fedoskino Factory Fund of Miniature Painting, village of Fedoskino, Mytishchi district, Moscow Region

RKF

Russkaya Kollektsia Fund, town of Dolgoprudny, Moscow Region

RLI

Russian Literature Institute (Pushkin House), St. Petersburg

PSMP

Peterhof State Museum Preserve, St. Petersburg

RPM

All-Russia Pushkin Museum, St. Petersburg

RMDAFA

All-Russia Museum of Decorative, Applied and Folk Art

Masterpieces of Russian Folk Art

Nadezhda Krestovskaya
Lacquer Miniatures. FEDOSKINO
Album

Director: *Gennady Popov*
Redactor: *Nadezhda Fedorova*
Computer lay-out: *Vladimir Bortnikov, Sergey Shilko*
Computer operator: *Konstantin Manov, Velentina Deviatkina*

The book has been prepared for publication by Interbook Business
Publishing license LR No 090012 August 15, 1991

Interbook Business has undertaken the publication
of the *Masterpieces of Russian Folk Art* series consisting
of handsomely designed art books on traditional Russian crafts.
An embodiment of the experience and talents of many
generations, folk crafts are constantly developing
and regenerating, thus remaining a viable modern
art which gives joy and beauty to the people.
Leading art critics and recognized master craftsmen have been
involved in the publication of the books of the present series.
Each book contains a survey of the history of the craft
and the work of prominent craftsmen, as well as about
150 illustrations, including the best works from both
Russian museums and private collections.

The following books of this series are in print:

I. Boguslavskaya
Painted Trays. Zhostovo

V. Borisova
Rostov Enamels

A. Kamorin
Lacquer Miniatures. Kholui

To establish cooperation and to purchase books, please, contact:
Interbook Business
Office 11, 12/9 Spiridonievsky Pereulok
Moscow, 103104, Russia
Phone: (095) 200-64-62
Fax: (095) 956-37-52